FAITH
UNFOLDED

YOUR DIVINE BLUEPRINT

PAUL DEZINNA

Faith Unfolded: Your Divine Blueprint

©2025 Copyright Paul DeZinna

ISBN: 979-8-9922828-0-1

PAUL DEZINNA
B O O K S

Paul DeZinna Books
Bethlehem, PA

INTRODUCTION

Paul DeZinna's message is deeply rooted in his Brooklyn upbringing, shaped by the borough's vibrant and diverse environment. This dynamic background infuses his teachings with authenticity and a unique perspective, reflecting the rich tapestry of cultures and experiences that define Brooklyn. Through his seven-week action plan devotional, Pauly draws on his foundation to connect with individuals from all walks of life, offering insights that resonate on a personal level. His approach is both grounded and inspired by his personal walk, inviting others to explore their own paths with courage and conviction. Growing up in the heart of Brooklyn, Paul witnessed firsthand the resilience and diversity of his community. These experiences have profoundly influenced his outlook on life and faith, enabling him to relate to people from various backgrounds with empathy and understanding. Paul's teachings are not only informed by his faith but also by the real-life challenges and triumphs he has encountered.

with a focus on practical and actionable steps, Paul's devotional guides individuals through life's complexities, helping them navigate their spiritual journey with confidence. His ability to draw parallels between everyday experiences and spiritual lessons makes his message accessible and relatable. Whether discussing the importance of staying true to one's values or the power of community and support, Paul's insights are both profound and pragmatic.

By blending his personal experiences with scriptural wisdom, he encourages others to reflect on their own journeys, fostering a deeper connection with their faith and purpose. His dedication to helping others discover their God-given potential is evident in every aspect of ministry. Through his teachings, Paul not only shares the message of God's love and guidance but also empowers individuals to live out their faith with intentionality and strength.

TABLE OF CONTENTS

Introduction 3

Week 1: Understanding Our Identity. 7

Week 2: Understanding God's Love 21

Week 3 Seeking the Lord 35

Week 4 Cultivating a Reverence for the Lord . 49

Week 5: Hearing the Shepherd's Voice 63

Week 6 Getting Uncomfortable 79

Week 7: Are You Ready? 93

- W E E K 1 -

UNDERSTANDING OUR IDENTITY

Key Verse:

Romans 8:17, NIV - "Now if we are children, then we are heirs—heirs of God and co-heirs with Christ, if indeed we share in his sufferings in order that we may also share in his glory."

- D A Y 1 -

KNOWING WHOSE YOU ARE

Reflection Step: As heirs of God, we have a sonship that cannot be taken away. Meditate on your identity in Christ and what it means to be an heir.

Action Step: Write down what it means to be a child of God. Share your thoughts with someone close to you.

Romans 8:17 - "Now if we are children, then we are heirs—heirs of God and co-heirs with Christ, if indeed we share in his sufferings in order that we may also share in his glory."

- DAY 2 -

EMBRACING SUFFERING

Reflection Step: Christ experienced trials and tribulations, and so will we. Reflect on *John 16:33*, where Jesus assures us of peace amidst tribulations.

Action Step: Identify a current struggle you're facing. Pray for strength to endure and write about how you can respond in faith rather than frustration.

- DAY 3 -

RESPONDING LIKE CHRIST

Reflection Step: Jesus responded to hurt and ridicule with love and grace. Consider how your responses reflect your faith.

Action Step: Choose one difficult relationship in your life. Make a conscious effort to respond with kindness and understanding this week.

Romans 8:17 - "Now if we are children, then we are heirs—heirs of God and co-heirs with Christ, if indeed we share in his sufferings in order that we may also share in his glory."

STANDING FIRM IN FAITH

Reflection Step: *Psalm 73:26* reminds us that God is our strength. Reflect on how you can stand firm in your faith during trials.

Action Step: Create a plan for daily prayer and Scripture reading to deepen your relationship with God. Commit to this plan for the week.

- D A Y 5 -

BEING THE LIGHT

Reflection Step: *Matthew 5:14* calls us to be the light of the world. How can your life reflect Christ to others?

Action Step: Identify one opportunity to share your faith or show kindness to someone this week. It could be a coworker, neighbor, or friend.

Romans 8:17 - "Now if we are children, then we are heirs—heirs of God and co-heirs with Christ, if indeed we share in his sufferings in order that we may also share in his glory."

- DAY 6 -

WALKING WITH INTEGRITY

Reflection Step: Integrity is crucial in our walk with Christ. Reflect on Proverbs and consider how integrity influences your decisions.

Action Step: Evaluate an area of your life where you might need to make a more ethical choice. Commit to taking action in that area this week.

- D A Y 7 -

CELEBRATING SMALL MIRACLES

Reflection Step: As we recognize God's blessings, we prepare ourselves for greater wonders. Reflect on the small miracles in your life.

Action Step: Spend time in gratitude. Write down at least three small miracles or blessings you've noticed this week and thank God for them.

Take the time to write down any areas you did not get to work on or felt you need to dig a little deeper into.

CLOSING PRAYER

Heavenly Father, thank You for making us heirs and co-heirs with Christ. Help us to embrace our identity and live in a way that reflects Your love and truth. Give us the strength to endure suffering, the light to shine in darkness, and the integrity to walk faithfully. May we recognize Your miracles in our lives, big and small. In Jesus's name, amen.

Author's Notes Based on Romans 8:17

"Now if we are children, then we are heirs—heirs of God and co-heirs with Christ, if indeed we share in his sufferings in order that we may also share in his glory."

Heirs: a person inheriting and continuing the legacy of a predecessor *(Oxford English Dictionary).*

As heirs of God, we have a sonship that cannot be taken away. We did not receive it based on our works. We did not receive it based on performance. We received the unconditional inheritance because God did what the law could not. He sent His one and only Son to live a sinless life and bear it all for us and our sins on the cross.

John 3:16 – "For God so loved the world, that he gave his only begot- ten Son, that whosoever believeth in him should not perish, but have everlasting life."

Co-heirs with Christ, we share the same inheritance of the kingdom that He shares. The spirit that raised Christ from the dead lives in each one of us.

Christ was fully man and experienced what we experienced but remained sinless.

When you say YES to Jesus and give up your old life to follow Jesus, there will be some hard times. The Word tells us that there will be trouble, trials, and tribulations and that we will be tested, but how we respond is key!

John 16:33 – "I have said these things to you, that in me you may have peace. In the world you will have tribulation. But take heart; I have overcome the world."

You will be hurt by some of the people closest to you.

Your character will be judged because you're going against the grain of the world.

You will be the topic of many conversations.

You will be ridiculed, called names, and labeled (Holy Roller).

Your character will be called into question when you begin to live a life that reflects one in the world, not of it.

Does this sound familiar?

Jesus went through all these things and still responded with truth, love, and grace.

He remained sinless and stayed away from slander, gossip, and retaliation.

I can honestly say that I have not always responded in that manner. If I was flying off the handle, walking around angry, and speaking ill of people who have hurt me at every chance, would I be a good witness of the Word?

Too many times, we want to take things into our own hands before consulting with God. I was told by a friend recently that I needed to fast and pray about what I was dealing with. The clarity begins when you start living your life with biblical principles and truth.

When we see the sufferings (trials) of our lives through biblical spectacles, it makes it easier for us to understand what we are going through and what is awaiting us.

Nothing worth something comes easy, right?

A college degree takes two to four years of studying. To be an athlete takes dedication and countless hours of practice, and to be great at your position at work takes training, hard work, and dedication.

Why should sharing in His glory be any different?

Paul writes in verse 18 that the present sufferings are nothing compared to the glory that will be revealed in us. When we actively seek God, yep, that is more than an hour on Sunday. He will reveal His glory in us and to us.

We need to be intentional about our relationship with God, and we need to seek HIM with a sense of urgency.

To my brothers in Christ, you need to understand that you are the head of your home; you are the pastor of your home, and God will hold YOU accountable for what you did NOT do to lead your family to Him. The times when you chose NOT to pray with your wife and the times when you chose divisive words to your children instead of life-breathing ones, He will hold you accountable.

Read *Ephesians 5:31:*

"Therefore, a MAN shall leave his father and mother and hold fast to his wife, and the two shall become one flesh."

A MAN shall leave, NOT a woman shall leave her parents. He has said it time and time again that it ALWAYS starts with the man.

Men, be bold in your walk with Christ, stand up for what is right, and oppose what is wrong.

We all have a lion inside of us. Let HIM ROAR! I want to encourage anyone who reads this.

We will see signs, miracles, and wonders in this life. In order to recognize these wonders, we have to be right with the LORD. Make sure to take note of the small miracles in your lives so that you may be able to grasp the wonders that are to come. We discredit the little miracles and blessings that God gives to us because our earthly view of what we want is different than what God knows we NEED.

There are a few ways to get through the sufferings that we may share in order to also share in His glory.

1-We Must Stand Firm

We have to stand firm in our faith to not wither when the trials and tribulations come. When you are growing closer to God, the Enemy will attack harder and harder, but God has given us everything to withstand the attacks. The Word of God tells us that we will go through trials and tribulations and hurts and pains, but HE is our strength. We will suffer as He suffered, but God's glory will be revealed when the dust settles.

Psalm 73:26:

"My health may fail, and my spirit may grow weak, but God remains the strength of my heart; he is mine forever."

2-Be the Light

We may be the only Bible that someone may see, so we have to behave that way. If trouble comes our way and we revert to the old ways of how we used to respond, how are we representing Christ?

Either at work or at home, we should behave the same way we would behave on a Sunday at church.

We will have some sandpaper people in our lives; those are the people who help burr the edges off us, as my friend and pastor used to say. We respond to them the same way by showing love, grace, and truth. If the season of that relationship is coming to an end, embrace it and know that God does not make mistakes.

Matthew 5:14:

"You are the light of the world"

Ephesians 5:8:

"For once you were full of darkness, but now you have light from the Lord. So live as people of light! For this light within you produces only what is good and right and true."

Psalm 73:26:

"My health may fail, and my spirit may grow weak, but God remains the strength of my heart; he is mine forever."

3-Walk with Integrity

Be a person of high morals and values. Every decision we make needs to be ethically correct and of integrity. Many times, we have to push our emotions aside and make the choice that is right in the eyes of God. Take the time to fast and pray to see where the Lord leads you. Walking with integrity is a way of life and is characterized

by honesty, moral uprightness, and consistency in the way we conduct ourselves. I have dealt with a lot of trouble in a certain area of my life, and I keep steadfast on walking with integrity because God will honor it and ultimately get the glory in the end.

Proverbs 11:3:

"The integrity of the upright guides them, but the unfaithful are destroyed by their duplicity."

Proverb 28:6:

"Better is a poor man who walks in his integrity Than a rich man who is twisted in his speech and is a shortsighted fool."

UNDERSTANDING GOD'S LOVE

Key Verse:

Malachi 1:2–3, NLT- "'I have always loved you,' says the Lord. But you retort, 'Really? How have you loved us?' And the Lord replies, 'This is how I showed my love for you: I loved your ancestor Jacob, but I rejected his brother, Esau, and devastated his hill country. I turned Esau's inheritance into a desert for jackals.'"

Malachi 1:2–3, NLT- "'I have always loved you,' says the Lord. But you retort, 'Really? How have you loved us?' And the Lord replies, 'This is how I showed my love for you: I loved your ancestor Jacob, but I rejected his brother, Esau, and devastated his hill country. I turned Esau's inheritance into a desert for jackals.'"

- DAY 1 -

GOD'S LOVE FOR YOU

Reflection Step: Think about God's declaration of love for His people, even in their doubts. Consider times in your life when you questioned God's love.

Action Step: Write a letter to God expressing your feelings and any doubts you've experienced. Acknowledge His love and faithfulness in your life.

Malachi 1:2–3, NLT- "'I have always loved you,' says the Lord. But you retort, 'Really? How have you loved us?' And the Lord replies, 'This is how I showed my love for you: I loved your ancestor Jacob, but I rejected his brother, Esau, and devastated his hill country. I turned Esau's inheritance into a desert for jackals.'"

- DAY 2 -

ACKNOWLEDGING OUR UNFAITHFULNESS

Reflection Step: The Israelites felt abandoned due to their circumstances. Reflect on areas in your life where unfaithfulness may be blocking your blessings.

Action Step: Identify one area of unfaithfulness in your life. Commit to making a change this week—whether in relationships, work, or personal habits. Write down three areas that you are intentionally going to work on.

Malachi 1:2–3, NLT- "'I have always loved you,' says the Lord. But you retort, 'Really? How have you loved us?' And the Lord replies, 'This is how I showed my love for you: I loved your ancestor Jacob, but I rejected his brother, Esau, and devastated his hill country. I turned Esau's inheritance into a desert for jackals.'"

- D A Y 3 -

RECOGNIZING OUR PRIORITIES

Reflection Step: God chose Jacob over Esau because of their differing priorities. Assess what you prioritize in your life. Write them down—godly or worldly desires?

Action Step: Make a list of things you value most. Pray over this list and ask God to help you shift your priorities to align with His will.

Malachi 1:2–3, NLT- "'I have always loved you,' says the Lord. But you retort, 'Really? How have you loved us?' And the Lord replies, 'This is how I showed my love for you: I loved your ancestor Jacob, but I rejected his brother, Esau, and devastated his hill country. I turned Esau's inheritance into a desert for jackals.'"

- DAY 4 -

REPENTANCE AND HUMILITY

Reflection Step: Repentance opens the door to healing and forgiveness. Reflect on *2 Chronicles 7:14* and what it means to humble yourself before God.

Action Step: Spend time in prayer, asking God to reveal areas where you need to repent. Write down specific actions you can take to turn away from those behaviors. Commit to turning away from those areas.

Malachi 1:2–3, NLT- "'I have always loved you,' says the Lord. But you retort, 'Really? How have you loved us?' And the Lord replies, 'This is how I showed my love for you: I loved your ancestor Jacob, but I rejected his brother, Esau, and devastated his hill country. I turned Esau's inheritance into a desert for jackals.'"

- DAY 5 -

DAILY COMMITMENT TO GOD

Reflection Step: Seek first the kingdom of God as we are commanded to do in *Matthew 6:33*. Consider how you can incorporate daily habits that draw you closer to Him.

Action Step: Establish a daily routine that includes Bible reading, prayer, and worship. Commit to this routine for the next week and track your progress (5/5/5 rule: read, pray, and worship for five minutes).

Malachi 1:2–3, NLT- "'I have always loved you,' says the Lord. But you retort, 'Really? How have you loved us?' And the Lord replies, 'This is how I showed my love for you: I loved your ancestor Jacob, but I rejected his brother, Esau, and devastated his hill country. I turned Esau's inheritance into a desert for jackals.'"

- DAY 6 -

ASSESSING INFLUENCES

Reflection Step: Reflect on the people, places, and things that influence your walk with God. Are they uplifting or dragging you down?

Action Step: Evaluate your relationships and activities. Choose to distance yourself from negative influences and seek out positive, godly friendships.

Malachi 1:2–3, NLT- "'I have always loved you,' says the Lord. But you retort, 'Really? How have you loved us?' And the Lord replies, 'This is how I showed my love for you: I loved your ancestor Jacob, but I rejected his brother, Esau, and devastated his hill country. I turned Esau's inheritance into a desert for jackals.'"

- DAY 7 -

SEEKING GOD'S PROTECTION

Reflection Step: Consider how your actions affect your relationship with God. Reflect on the importance of His protection over your life.

Action Step: Spend time in prayer, asking for God's protection over you and your family. Write down practical steps you can take to strengthen your relationship with Him.

CLOSING PRAYER

Thank You, Lord, for allowing me the opportunity this week to focus on You. Lord, allow me to reflect this week on the areas in my life that need to sharpen from this week's devotional. Thank You for Your grace and mercy. In Jesus's name, I pray, amen.

Author's Notes Based on Malachi 1:2–3

"'I have always loved you,' says the Lord, but you retort, 'Really? How have you loved us?' And the Lord replies, 'This is how I showed my love for you: I loved your ancestor Jacob, but I rejected his brother, Esau, and devastated his hill country. I turned Esau's inheritance into a desert for the jackals.'"

When you look at this Scripture and try to apply it to your life, you have to understand it a little more.

The word retort means to answer back sharply or angry (Oxford Languages).

The Israelites were a little upset because they felt that God did not love them anymore, but the Lord was letting them know that they were His chosen people. He blessed their ancestor Jacob with a double portion of his inheritance, and God changed Jacob's name to Israel, whom they were named after. God didn't stop loving them. They were failing to understand that, due to their unfaithfulness, their blessings were blocked.

How many of us have felt the same way that the Israelites did?

God, You don't love me anymore. If You did, why would this be happening to me?

God, why didn't I get that promotion at work? (While you're flirting with every person you meet).

God, why is the Enemy attacking all the relationships in my life? (When you're spending more time with Jack Daniels, Johnny Walker, and the boys at work than pouring into your relationships at home.)

God will not bless your circumstances if you are not faithful!

We serve a forgiving God, a loving God, and a merciful God, but we also serve a jealous God!

He is not going to bless you if you have other gods in your life: money, porn, drugs, alcohol, and so on.

We know that God is love, and God is unchanging, so when He said that he rejected Esau, it does not mean that He did not love him; he just preferred Jacob over Esau.

Why did God prefer Jacob over Esau? Esau loved the things of this world, and Jacob didn't.

Jacob was a simple man, and even though he had sinned by cheating his brother out of his birthright, God still used him.

Never think it's too late for God to be able to use you. God will take our mistakes and turn them into miracles!

We must take our feet out of the world; enough is enough! We must stop being lukewarm Christians!

The second coming of Christ will be here, and we need to get right with God!

When we look at the last part of the Scripture, it says that He turned the hill country into a desert for the jackals.

If you do a bit more of a deep dive into this, it was prophesied that the city of Edom would be abandoned. Due to their sins and their unfaithfulness, the favor of God was not upon them, and destruction would come.

Ezekiel 28:13-19:

I'm not sure about anyone else, but I do not want to lose God's protection over my family and myself because of my love of the world, and my unfaithfulness to Him. More importantly, I do not want the relationship between the Lord and myself to be strained or affected because I was not doing what I needed to do as a man of God.

What are a few simple ways of getting right with God?

- Guard what you are putting in your mind. Garbage in, garbage out.
- The shows that we are watching must change.

They are loaded with sex, the love of money, drugs, and so many other ungodly things.

This is strategic, and the Enemy knows that we fall for it. We sing lyrics that we don't understand and watch things that eventually take root in our hearts and minds.

- Going out on a Friday to the pub and putting down a pint of Guinness—yep, that must stop!
- Gossiping with your coworkers, friends, and family—yep, that must stop!

I always remind myself of people, places, and things. These are some of the things that will trip up your walk with God: the people you spend time with, the places that you go, and the things that you take part in.

Those were the simple activities that we can change in our lives to see a difference in our walk with the Lord and a difference in ourselves.

There are a few things that we must do in order to get right with God.

1-Repentance

We are called to repent for our sins. Have that honest conversation with God and humbly ask Him for forgiveness. When we repent, we must turn from that sin and sin no more.

2 Chronicles 7:14:

"If my people who are called by my name will humble themselves, and pray and seek my face, and turn from their wicked ways, then I will hear from heaven, and will forgive their sin and heal their land."

2-Read Your Bible Daily

In order to know what God's will for your life is, you need to get to know God, and the way to do that is to read His Word daily. The Bible is filled from front to back with wisdom, knowledge, expectations, and purpose.

It is a road map to life. I have heard someone explain it this way: Basic Instructions Before Leaving Earth.

2 Timothy 3:16:

"All Scripture is breathed out by God and profitable for teaching, for reproof, for correction and for training in righteousness."

3-Pray Daily

This is a conversation with you and God. It does not have to sound fancy and as if it belongs on a podcast. He knows your heart; just speak to Him. I used to overcomplicate this. It needed to be the right time, place, weather, and anything I could use as an excuse. I didn't make the excuse because I didn't want to pray; I made the excuse

because I overthought the whole thing and was nervous. I felt as if I needed to sound like the elders in my prayer circle or the guys on YouTube, but I needed to just be real with my Father in heaven.

1 Thessalonians:5:16-18

"Always be joyful. Never stop praying. Be thankful in all circumstances, for this is God's will for you who belong to Christ Jesus."

SEEKING THE LORD

Key Verse:

Psalm 34:10 NLT- "Even strong young lions sometimes go hungry, but those who trust in the Lord will lack no good thing."

- D A Y 1 -

UNDERSTANDING SEEKING

Reflection Step: To seek the Lord means to intentionally desire His presence and guidance. Reflect on what it means to genuinely seek Him in your life.

Action Step: Write a prayer expressing your desire to seek God wholeheartedly this week.

- D A Y 2 -

DISCERNING NEEDS VS. WANTS

Reflection Step: God promises to provide for our needs, not necessarily our wants. Consider the difference in your prayers. Are you seeking God for His provision or just for what you want?

Action Step: Make a list of your needs and wants. Focus your prayers this week on seeking God for your true needs.

- D A Y 3 -

SHUTTING OUT THE NOISE

Reflection Step: Just as David turned to music in his troubles (1 Sam. 16:23), we need to eliminate distractions to hear God's voice. What noise is distracting you from seeking Him?

Action Step: Choose one secular activity (like a TV show or music) to reduce or eliminate this week. Replace that time with prayer or worship.

- D A Y   4 -

ALONE TIME WITH GOD

Reflection Step: When you read *Ecclesiastes 3:7*, *"A time to tear and a time to mend. A time to be quiet and a time to speak,"* it clearly tells you that silence and solitude can open your heart to hear God. How often do you spend quiet time with Him?

Action Step: Carve out at least ten to fifteen minutes daily this week for quiet prayer or meditation. Reflect on what God reveals to you during this time. Write down what is revealed to you in your quiet time.

- DAY 5 -

FINDING A MENTOR

Reflection Step: A spiritual mentor can guide and challenge you in your walk with Christ. Have you sought guidance from someone with more experience?

Action Step: Ask God to help you identify a potential mentor or two in your life. Reach out to them and ask if they are willing to support you in your spiritual journey.

- DAY 6 -

HUMBLING YOURSELF

Reflection Step: *James 4:10 says, "Humble yourselves before the Lord, and he will lift you up in honor."* Humility is essential for growth. Are you open to feedback and corrections from others?

Action Step: Reflect on an area where you may need to humble yourself. Consider how accepting guidance can lead to spiritual growth.

Psalm 34:10 - "Even strong young lions sometimes go hungry, but those who trust in the Lord will lack no good thing."

- DAY 7 -

COMMITTING TO SEEK

Reflection Step: Seeking the Lord is a lifelong commitment that brings peace and fulfillment. How will you continue to prioritize seeking Him?

Action Step: Create a plan for how you will seek the Lord regularly. This could include daily prayer, reading Scripture, praying with a friend or loved one, or meeting with your mentor. Write down your commitment and share it with someone for accountability.

CLOSING PRAYER

Heavenly Father, thank You for the promise that those who seek You will lack no good thing. Help us to be intentional in our pursuit of You in Jesus's name, amen.

Author's Notes Based on Psalm 34:10

"The lions may grow weak and hungry, but those who seek the Lord lack no good thing."

Seek: attempt to find or a desire to obtain or achieve. Desire: strongly wish for or want something

Let's wordplay for a few.

The lions may grow weak and hungry, but those who desire to obtain the Lord lack no good thing.

(Seek)

The lions may grow weak and hungry, but those who strongly want the Lord lack no good thing.

(Desire)

Our Creator is an artist with His words, and every word He speaks is on purpose, so please do not take them lightly.

A lion is considered the dominant one in the jungle. He is big in stature, strength, and boldness.

Once again, God is painting a picture with His words. He is giving us this image to see in our minds of this miraculous animal being hungry and weak. BUT when we envision the next part of the Scripture, we see ourselves lacking nothing we need and having an abundant life because we seek after Him as we build our foundation on HIM.

When the Scriptures say, "lack no good thing," it refers to what we need in life, not what we want.

Many times, we get those two things confused. Jesus is not a genie that we can use to grant us wishes. I used to think that every time

I needed something, I could just pray and walk away.

The Scriptures tell us that we have to be intentional about seeking the Lord. Your heart has to want it, or you will not receive what He has for you.

I went to church in Brooklyn plenty of times, but I was not seeking the Lord, so I did not receive what God had in store for me. I could just imagine in my head the amount of blessings that God had for me, but I missed them because my heart wasn't postured correctly. I was not living for Him; I was living for myself.

It wasn't until I made the decision to follow, seek, and desire Him to be part of my everyday life that I began to see how clear God's love for me was. I began to see the moments where I was dealing with something and God's hand began to move in that situation.

I am not a Bible scholar, so I decided to look up how many times the Bible says we should seek the Lord—I stopped at forty.

Here are a few that you can look up and study.

Acts 15:16–17; Psalm 27:8; Isaiah 55:6–7; and Proverbs 8:17

In my early walk, I didn't pray or worship much. I did the bare minimum, and that was NOT working. I needed to do something different. I needed to do what my wife did, and that was to be all in and seek Him daily.

My plan of action that I want to share with you when I needed to refocus and be all in seeking the Lord is:

1–Shut Out the Noise

I had to cut off all secular (earthly) things. That means TV shows, movies, music, and so much more. I can tell you that ALL these things I mentioned are laced with sin and created with the purpose of infiltrating your mind. The creators are strategic with what they want you to hear, see, and think. You cannot turn on anything that doesn't have sex, drugs, cursing, or a dozen other things that we should not be allowing access to our minds. What we allow in shapes how we talk, how we act, and how we begin to live our lives. When we hit a roadblock in life, how do you think we will handle it after allowing all of these toxic things into our minds? I wanted to be like David when I had tribulations in my life.

1 Samuel 16:23:

"And whenever the tormenting spirit from God troubled Saul, David would play the harp. Then Saul would feel better, and the tormenting spirit would go away."

2-Have Alone Time with God

Take the time to just sit in the presence of God. Carve out some quiet time to pray and worship.

I needed to sit in silence and allow Him to just speak to me. It wasn't an audible voice; it was a nudge He would put on my heart that allowed me to know His will for me. On the way to work, I would keep the radio off and just listen to see where He led me. When we sit quiet long enough, eliminate the distractions, and create an atmosphere to allow God to speak to us, He will.

Ecclesiastes 3:7:

"A time to tear and a time to mend,

A time to be silent and a time to speak."

3-Get a Spiritual Mentor

This one is important. We have to find someone who meets a few different qualifications. The person we ask to take on this responsibility has to be:

> 1-Grounded in God's Word and spiritually and emotionally healthy. I never said perfect because I would have never found my mentor. A perfect person doesn't exist

> 2-Willing to spend one-on-one time with you and go through life helping you in your walk with Christ.

> 3-Willing to tell you what you need to hear, not what you want to hear.

I had to humble myself to accept what was said to me. This could have been good, bad, or indifferent. No one likes to be told that they are doing something wrong or need to change how they are doing something that they've probably been doing their whole life.

We need this person in our lives to tell us the things that we need to hear, not things that we want to hear, and help us see areas in our lives that are not in alignment with God's Word.

When you don't know, you don't know, and your spiritual mentor can help you course correct.

Proverbs 15:27:

"Plans go wrong for lack of advice; many advisers bring success."

Proverbs 19:20, NLT

"Get all the advice and instruction you can, so you will be wise the rest of your life."

- WEEK 4 -

CULTIVATING A REVERENCE FOR THE LORD

Key Verse:

Psalm 19:9, NLT – "Reverence for the Lord is pure, lasting forever. The laws of the Lord are true; each one is fair."

- D A Y 1 -

UNDERSTANDING REVERENCE

Reflection Step: Reverence means treating God with deep respect. His laws are pure, true, and fair, lasting forever.Consider what it means to honor God in your daily life.

Action Step: Write down three ways you can show reverence to God this week. Take the time to put them into action.

- DAY 2 -

THE IMPORTANCE OF OBEDIENCE

Reflection Step: God values obedience over sacrifice. Reflect on your current obedience to God's Word and promptings. Reflect on this verse in *1 Samuel 15:22*. Are there areas where you resist His guidance?

Action Step: Spend time in prayer, asking God for wisdom in a particular situation. Write down what He reveals to you.

- D A Y 3 -

SEEKING WISDOM

Reflection Step: Wisdom comes from the Lord and helps us navigate life's challenges. Think about decisions you've maderecently—did you seek God's wisdom?

Action Step: Spend time in prayer, asking God for wisdom in a particular situation. Write down what He reveals to you.

- D A Y 4 -

TRUSTING IN GOD

Reflection Step: Trusting God means relying on His understanding rather than our own. Read and meditate on Proverbs 3:5–6 and recall a time when trusting Him changed your situation for the better.

Action Step: Write a prayer of trust, laying your worries before God. Commit to trusting Him with a specific issue this week.

- DAY 5 -

GRATITUDE FOR HIS LOVE

Reflection Step: God's faithful love endures forever. Reflect on the ways God has shown you His love, even during difficult times.

Action Step: Create a gratitude list of at least five ways God has been faithful to you. Share this list with someone to encourage them.

- D A Y 6 -

AVOIDING DISTRACTION

Reflection Step: We live in a world overloaded with information that can confuse and divide. Consider what distractions are pulling you away from God.

Action Step: Action Step: Identify one source of distraction (e.g., social media, news) and limit your exposure this week. Spend that time in prayer or reading the Bible instead.

- DAY 7 -

SHARING WISDOM WITH OTHERS

Reflection Step: God gives wisdom generously to those who ask. This is not a secret; refer to *James 1:5* and see that it is for all of us. Think about how you can share the wisdom you've gained from your walk with Christ.

Action Step: Reach out to someone in need of guidance this week. Offer them support and share a lesson you've learned about reverence for God.

CLOSING PRAYER

Heavenly Father, thank You for your eternal truth and love. Help us cultivate a deeper reverence for You in our hearts and actions. May we be obedient, wise, and trusting as we navigate our daily lives. In Jesus's name, amen.

Author's Notes Based on Psalm 19:9 NLT

"Reverence for the Lord is pure, lasting forever. The laws of the Lord are true; each one is fair."

Sometimes, we read Scripture and do not understand what a word means or the verse, so I like to check the meanings of the words used.

Reverence: Treat with deep respect.

Pure: Spotless, stainless, free from dust, dirt or taint.

This verse is saying that a deep respect for the Lord is spotless and free from taint, lasting forever. His laws and judgments are true and righteous. It follows up by saying in verse 10 that these laws are more desirable than gold, even the finest gold.

I must be H.O.T. (honest, open, and transparent). Today, there are too many people lacking a reverence for the Lord, including some brothers and sisters in Christ. We are humans, and we like to walk that thin line of being in the world and being in the church. We think that God's grace and mercy is a get-out-of-jail-free card. We all know that we serve a loving God, a forgiving God. BUT we are still must answer for ALL we have done. No matter the good, bad, or indifferent, we will appear before the judgment seat of Christ.

2 Corinthians 5:10:

"For we must all appear before the judgment seat of Christ, so that each of us may receive what is due us for the things done while in the body, whether good or bad."

We must have a Christ-centered mindset so we can eliminate some of the bad decisions we will have to answer for.

When we say reverence for the Lord, it is said in the context of fear for the Lord. It is not a fear in the sense of scary fear but more of a healthy fear as one has for his or her parents.

I personally think back on some of the times I made decisions without Christ, and I shake my head. I can remember times when I led people to sin, and it breaks my heart that I was the one who was used by the Enemy as a stumbling block for someone else. I thank God that His love is unconditional, and He loved me when I was unlovable.

1 Chronicles 16:34:

"Give thanks to the Lord, for he is good! His faithful love endures forever."

When we make decisions and attempt to do things on our own and do not get the result we want, we tend to get upset and have our pity parties. When we are in the Word of God, and we operate under His guidance, we have peace when things don't go according to our plan. We know that we serve a big God, and His plan and purpose are greater than we can imagine. As you mature in your walk with Christ and you put your faith in HIM, you know that His decisions are just and fair.

The Scripture that follows says that His laws are more desirable than gold, even the finest gold. It is sweeter than honey dropping from the comb. They are a warning to your servant.

When you receive a warning, that usually means something is about to happen, right?

So, you're telling me that when I obey Him, He is going to hook me up and keep me out of trouble. He is going to warn me to run, get out, or not to go down that road. This is a no-brainer for me on what decision I am to make. God usually gives us an out before we do something stupid, and it's our job to take it.

Look at the wisdom that you get as well. You now know how to navigate certain waters because God led you through whatever it was. It is your job to share that wisdom with others. God's blessings continue to reach others because of your obedience.

Why don't we have reverence for the Lord the way we used to? What changed?

We have too much information at our fingertips. We are overloaded with all these social media outlets, news, podcasts, YouTubers, and much more. Everyone's an expert on everything now, and they feel they need to share their opinions. More than most are all opinion-based and NOT factual. All that info is confusing people and causing division. We were never meant to process all this information.

Genesis 2:17:

"But you must not eat from the tree of the knowledge of good and evil, for when you eat from it you will certainly die."

The Enemy is slick because he uses the overloading of information to get us confused and cause division in our homes, our jobs, and even the church.

I am personally dealing with this on multiple levels in my own home. I have teenagers and the amount of confusion on how they are to look, eat, or act based on what the world says. I am teaching them that what this world tells them is a lie, and we focus on what the Word tells us!

How can we live out Psalm 19:9?

1–Obedience

We must be obedient to God's Word, His promptings (the Holy Spirit), and His teachings.

Being dependent on the Holy Spirit to lead us in the path of obedience is part of our walk with Christ. When God prompts us to do something or He leads us somewhere, we need to say yes because everything He leads us to and through is on purpose and for a purpose.

Believe me, it is not easy at times being in the world and not of it. We will have to be the oddball out in the world's eyes, and we have to be okay with that. I have been in plenty of instances where the people around me were behaving one way, and I had to excuse myself from their presence.

1 Samuel 15:22:

"But Samuel replied, 'What is more pleasing to the Lords; your burnt offerings and sacrifices or your obedience to his voice? Listen, obedience

is better than sacrifice and submission is better than offering the fat of rams.'"

2-Wisdom/Discernment

The definition of wisdom is the quality or state of being wise; knowledge of what is true or right coupled with just judgment as to action, sagacity, discernment, or insight (Dictionary.com).

When we read God's Word, it makes us wise beyond our years. Wisdom helps us from making the same mistake twice. When you are wise, you see things differently because you already have insight to something similar that has happened in your life.

Using wisdom and discernment in our choices is key. If we know that something will hinder our walk with Christ or something will cause division and hurt in a relationship, we must use wisdom and NOT put ourselves in those situations.

3-Trust

We must trust that He is who He says He is. He is the almighty healer, the one who ransomed His life for ours. I had to trust that HE was the one who would pull me out of a life that was full of sin and shaped me to who I am today. I had to trust that He was the one who was going to repair my marriage, heal my daughter, and supply for my every need. It is a must that we trust that His love endures forever. We serve a powerful God and have to trust when He says that nothing we lay before His feet is too big for Him.

Proverbs 3:5−6:

"Trust in the Lord with all your heart; do not depend on your own understanding."

Psalm 136:1:

"Give thanks to the Lord, for he is good! His faithful love endures forever."

HEARING THE SHEPHERD'S VOICE

Key Verse:

John: 10:10, NIV – "The thief comes only to steal, kill and destroy. I have come that they may have life and have it to the full."

John: 10:10, NIV - "The thief comes only to steal, kill and destroy. I have come that they may have life and have it to the full."

- D A Y   1 -

UNDERSTANDING THE THIEF

Reflection Step: The "thief" represents false shepherds who promise life outside of Christ. Reflect on any influences that may be leading you away from Jesus. Who or what are the "thieves" in your life?

Action Step: Pray for discernment to identify false influences in your life. Write down one area where you feel you are being misled and bring it to God.

64 | FAITH UNFOLDED: YOUR DIVINE BLUEPRINT

- D A Y 2 -

THE TRUE SHEPHERD

Reflection Step: Jesus is not playing when it comes to His people. Reading *Ezekiel 34:10*, it is written, *"This is what the Sovereign Lord says: I am against the shepherds and will hold them accountable."*

Action Step: Jesus, our true Shepherd, cares deeply for His flock. How does this realization change your understanding of His leadership in your life?

John: 10:10, NIV - "The thief comes only to steal, kill and destroy. I have come that they may have life and have it to the full."

LISTENING TO THE SHEPHERD'S VOICE

Reflection Step: The "thief" represents false shepherds who promise life outside of Christ. Reflect on any influences that may be leading you away from Jesus. Who or what are the "thieves" in your life?

Action Step: Pray for discernment to identify false influences in your life. Write down one area where you feel you are being misled and bring it to God.

John: 10:10, NIV - "The thief comes only to steal, kill and destroy. I have come that they may have life and have it to the full."

- D A Y 4 -

THE IMPORTANCE
OF QUIET TIME

Reflection Step: Reflect on how time spent in God's Word illuminates your path.Has your decisions been guided by this Scripture recently? *(Psalm 119:105).*

Action Step: Create a dedicated space for daily quiet time. Commit to reading a chapter from the Bible each day this week, reflecting on how it speaks to your life.

- DAY 5 -

BUILDING A RELATIONSHIP

Reflection Step: Just as you prioritize relationships with family and friends, prioritize your relationship with God. What steps can you take to deepen this connection?

Action Step: Schedule a regular time each week for intimate conversations with God, similar to a date with a loved one. Write down your thoughts and prayers.

John: 10:10, NIV - "The thief comes only to steal, kill and destroy. I have come that they may have life and have it to the full."

UNDERSTANDING SCRIPTURE

Reflection Step: The importance of understanding Scripture cannot be overstated. Are you simply checking off a box or truly engaging with God's Word?

Action Step: Choose a passage you've read recently and research its context. Share your findings with a friend or mentor to foster discussion.

John: 10:10, NIV - "The thief comes only to steal, kill and destroy. I have come that they may have life and have it to the full."

- DAY 7 -

REJOICING IN THE SHEPHERD'S CARE

Reflection Step: Jesus actively seeks us when we wander. Reflect on a time you felt lost and how you were brought back into His fold.

Action Step: Write a prayer of thanksgiving for His relentless pursuit of you. Consider reaching out to someone who may feel lost, and offer them encouragement or support.

CLOSING PRAYER

Dear Lord, thank You for being our true Shepherd. Help us to discern Your voice amidst the noise of the world. Guide us to deeper understanding and intimacy with You. Amen.

Author's Notes Based on John 10:10

"The thief comes only to steal, kill and destroy. I have come that they may have life and have it to the full."

Thief: A person who steals, especially secretly or without open force.

When we read this text or we hear a sermon on it, we all think that it means the thief is the Enemy (Satan).

As I dug into this verse and did research, I realized it is not the case. In this specific verse, Jesus referred to the shepherds of Israel as the thief. He was talking about the false prophets. Anyone who came before our great shepherd, Jesus Christ, and promised us an abundant life in anything besides following Jesus is a thief.

A thief is someone who is for self-gain. BUT Jesus is selfless.

To gain Christ as our Shepherd is the greatest thing that can happen to us.

Jesus speaks about shepherds who only take care of themselves. He talks about them eating good and getting fat while the flock is left to the wild with no protection. Jesus, the sovereign Lord, states that He is against them, and He holds them accountable for His flock. Jesus does not take lightly when His flock is not cared for properly. The shepherds who did not shepherd the flock well will be dealt with accordingly as per the Scriptures. There is a lot of Scripture to share, but I want to encourage you to read *Ezekiel 34*.

In the book of Jeremiah, Jesus called out those who tended to his sheep (us) and had not done a good job. He told them that He would bestow punishment on them for the evil they had done.

Jeremiah 23:1−2:,NIV

"'Woe to the shepherds who are destroying and scattering the sheep of my pasture!' declares the LORD. Therefore this is what the LORD, the God of Israel, says to the shepherds who tend my people: 'Because you have scattered my flock and driven them away and have not bestowed care on them, I will bestow punishment on you for the evil you have done,' declares the LORD."

Jesus tells us that He will gather the remnant of His flock from ALL countries and bring them back to pastures, where they will be fruitful. He says that there will be from different herds but will become one.

Like a sheep knows the shepherd's voice, we are to know our Shepherd's voice. When the Shepherd calls on the flock, they will follow His commands; they will obey His directions. If the sheep do not listen to the Shepherd, they will fall prey to the wild animals, and they will eat things that they can NOT eat.

As Christ followers and children of God, we must listen to our Shepherd's voice so we do not fall prey to this world and the dangers that lie ahead. Our Lord's commands are to save us from trouble and keep us from going down roads and paths that are not good for us.

When we wander off and can be headed for trouble, His voice can bring us home and keep us safe.

When we wander and are not in connection with the Shepherd, and when His voice is faint because we are farther away from him, other things can begin to lead us, guide us, and we can allow those things

to control our lives. This is how Satan works; he whispers in your ear, and before you know it, his voice is louder and louder, drowning out the voice of your true Shepherd. When we have wandered from the flock, we have found ourselves in some dark places. The Enemy wants to keep us there because when we are living in the dark, we are full of shame and are afraid to come out. Our Shepherd cares deeply for us. He will rejoice when we are found, so step out of the dark and into the light so that He may rescue you!

Matthew 18:12−14:

"If a man has a hundred sheep and one of them wanders away, what will he do? Won't he leave the ninety-nine others on the hills and go out to search for the one that is lost? And if he finds it, I tell you the truth, he will rejoice over it more than over the ninety-nine that didn't wander away!"

When we hear our Shepherd's voice, we follow Him and obey His commands, just like the sheep do. Why do you think we and the sheep obey and follow their Shepherd?

It is the bond that was formed between the two. It was the intimate relationship we have with one another. It is the trust that our Shepherd will guide us and lead us according to the will of God.

It warns us that attacks will happen and troubles will come. BUT the Shepherd will not abandon us like the hired hand will if the wolves come. The great Shepherd will lead us to safety. He will protect us; He will be a lamp to our feet and a light for our path to safety.

Psalm 119:105:

"Your word is a lamp for my feet, a light on my path." Light is something that is necessary to navigate this world of darkness. We need light to guide us safely through the unforeseen dangers that await us.

God gave us two ears and one mouth for a reason. He wants us to be still and listen.

He wants us to listen intently to His voice. We should hang onto every word spoken to us by our Shepherd.

When I allowed my ego or flesh to win and I decided that my way was better than HIS way, it never worked out in my favor. We must put all our trust in Him; we need to surrender daily to our flesh and our own will. We must accept Him as our Lord and Savior, and our ways must be His ways.

Romans 10:9–10:

"If you declare with your mouth, 'Jesus is Lord,' and believe in your heart that God raised him from the dead, you will be saved. For it is with your heart that you believe and are justified, and it is with your mouth that you profess your faith and are saved."

If we start digging into some cross-referencing Scripture, Jesus was calling out the shepherds of Israel; He was calling out the people He allowed to shepherd His people. He called out the shepherds who were only for profit.

Jeremiah 23:1−2

Anyone who tries to lead people away from Jesus and tries to hinder their salvation is the thief!

John 10:9:

"I am the gate: whoever enters through me will be saved. They will come in and go out and find pastures. Jesus is the way, the truth and the life and the only way to the father is through HIM."

John 14:6:

"Jesus answered, I am the way and the truth and the life. No one comes to the father except through me."

To be honest, I was all over the place with this verse, and for so long, I was misled, thinking that the thief was only the Enemy.

How do we come to know our Shepherd's voice?

1-Quiet Time/Quality Time with Him

This means that you must silence everything. Turn off the phones and television.

Dedicate a place to go with no distractions and just have your alone time with God.

If your mind starts to drift (and it may), reset and refocus so that your quiet time with God is not hindered.

Many times, we believe that we need to sound like a megachurch pastor when we pray, but that is the furthest thing from the truth. Do not over spiritualize it. Enjoy the intimate conversation with your heavenly Father. When you are consistent with your

quiet time with God, His voice will become clear to you.

When we are intentional with sitting with someone in private so that we may have an uninterrupted conversation, the conversations are deeper and more intimate. The other person will share

Their heart, and you can do the same. We learn things about the person we are sitting with and vice versa.

My son and I take time every so often to go out for chicken fingers and ice cream. We get to sit in a quiet booth and have deep-rooted conversations. He gets to share with me what is going on in his life (we think we know, but we don't), and I get to share things I am dealing with. We get to talk about plans we have or want to make; these conversations are so beneficial to our relationship. When you take the time out to have that one-on-one time with God, your spouse, your children, or brother/sister in Christ, the relationship grows and flourishes.

The conversations didn't just happen. I prioritized my time with my son. I was intentional about carving this time out for him and me to have this quality time together.

Our relationship with our Lord and Savior must be the same way:

1-A priority

2-Intentional

3-Of quality

4-Intimate

5-Personal

2-Read Scripture to Understand the Scripture

I like to explain it like this:

Some people listen to respond versus listening to hear.

There are times when we run through a quick couple of verses to not lose our streak on the Bible app, or we are just trying to check off the box to say, I read my Bible today. We are all guilty at one point or another of doing it.

We like to grab a few parts of a verse and use it where it will benefit us, but we really have zero clue what it means. The scary thing is that when we do that, we share with others, and they start believing and sharing, and before you know it, a ton of people are using Scripture in the wrong context because it was used wrong or for the wrong reasons.

It is good to dig into the Scripture that you are studying. Do a little research on the book you're reading. Go online and see what a particular verse means. I like to watch sermons on YouTube based on some Scripture I am reading. A good way to gain insight and knowledge of a Scripture is to link up with your spiritual mentor or fellow believer and ask questions. The more you understand the Word, the closer you get to Him and the clearer the Shepherd's voice becomes.

GETTING UNCOMFORTABLE

Key Verse:

Judges 6:13, AMP – "But Gideon said to him, 'Please my Lord, if the Lord is with us, then why has all this happened to us? And where are all His wondrous works which our fathers told us about when they said, "Did not the Lord bring us up from Egypt?" But now the Lord has abandoned us and put us into the hand of Midian.'"

Judges 6:13, AMP - "But Gideon said to him, 'Please my Lord, if the Lord is with us, then why has all this happened to us? And where are all His wondrous works which our fathers told us about when they said, "Did not the Lord bring us up from Egypt?" But now the Lord has abandoned us and put us into the hand of Midian.'"

- D A Y 1 -

RECOGNIZING OUR IDOLS

Reflection Step: Reflect on Gideon's question to God about His presence amid adversity. Just as the Israelites worshiped false gods, we often let modern-day idols take God's place in our lives. Identify what distracts you from your relationship with Him.

Action Step: Write down three things that may have become idols in your life (e.g., sports, social media, materialism). Spend time in prayer, asking God to reveal other areas where you may need to refocus. Write down the items identified so they are visible to you.

Judges 6:13, AMP - "But Gideon said to him, 'Please my Lord, if the Lord is with us, then why has all this happened to us? And where are all His wondrous works which our fathers told us about when they said, "Did not the Lord bring us up from Egypt?" But now the Lord has abandoned us and put us into the hand of Midian.'"

- DAY 2 -

ACCOUNTABILITY FOR OUR ACTIONS

Reflection Step: Like the Israelites, we can often blame external factors for our struggles. Take responsibility for your decisions and the consequences they bring.

Action Step: Reflect on a recent challenge you faced. Write down how you contributed to that situation. Pray for guidance on how to make better choices moving forward.

Judges 6:13, AMP - "But Gideon said to him, 'Please my Lord, if the Lord is with us, then why has all this happened to us? And where are all His wondrous works which our fathers told us about when they said, "Did not the Lord bring us up from Egypt?" But now the Lord has abandoned us and put us into the hand of Midian.'"

- DAY 3 -

CHALLENGING OUR COMFORT ZONES

Reflection Step: Change can be uncomfortable. Are you willing to leave behind the habits and relationships that hinder your walk with Christ?

Action Step: Identify one unhealthy relationship or habit to address this week. Plan a conversation or a decision to step away. Pray for strength and clarity. Reach out to your spiritual mentor if necessary.

- D A Y   4 -

SEEING OURSELVES AS GOD SEES US

Reflection Step: Gideon doubted his worthiness despite being called a mighty warrior. Read *Deuteronomy 28:13*, *"If you listen to these commands of the Lord your God that I am giving you today, and if you carefully obey them, the Lord will make you the head and not the tail, and you will always be on top and never at the bottom."*

How do you see yourself in light of God's truth?

Action Step: Write down affirmations based on Scripture (e.g., 1 John 3–1; 2 Cor. 5:17). Recite these affirmations daily to reinforce your identity in Christ.

- D A Y   5 -

DAILY PRAYER PRACTICE

Reflection Step: *Philippians 4:6–7* tells us to bring your requests to God through prayer, and we will experience His peace. Prayer is a conversation with your Creator. Are you making time to speak with God daily?

Action Step: Start and end your day with a simple prayer. List three things you're grateful for each morning and three struggles to share with God each night.

Judges 6:13, AMP - "But Gideon said to him, 'Please my Lord, if the Lord is with us, then why has all this happened to us? And where are all His wondrous works which our fathers told us about when they said, "Did not the Lord bring us up from Egypt?" But now the Lord has abandoned us and put us into the hand of Midian.'"

- DAY 6 -

ENGAGING WITH THE WORD

Reflection Step: How often are you engaging with Scripture? Are you allowing God's Word to transform your heart and mind?

Action Step: Commit to reading at least one verse a day. Use a Bible app or devotional to help you stay consistent. Journal your thoughts and any changes you notice in your life.

Judges 6:13, AMP - "But Gideon said to him, 'Please my Lord, if the Lord is with us, then why has all this happened to us? And where are all His wondrous works which our fathers told us about when they said, "Did not the Lord bring us up from Egypt?" But now the Lord has abandoned us and put us into the hand of Midian.'"

- DAY 7 -

FINDING ACCOUNTABILITY

Reflection Step: Accountability can be challenging but is essential for spiritual growth. One of the key Scriptures you will hear is *Proverbs 27:17: "Iron sharpens iron, and one person sharpens another."*

Who can you turn to for support and encouragement?

Action Step: Identify an accountability partner—someone rooted in faith and aligned with your values. Set a time to meet weekly or biweekly to discuss your spiritual goals and struggle.

CLOSING PRAYER

Heavenly Father, As I move through this week, I commit to evaluating my life in light of God's Word and acknowledge idols, seeking accountability and embracing my identity as a valued heir of Christ. Lord, I trust that as I prioritize my relationship with You, I will witness Your wondrous works in my life. In Jesus's name, amen.

Author's Notes Based on Judges 6:13

"But Gideon said to him, 'Please my lord, if the Lord is with us, then why has all this happened to us? And where are all His wondrous works which our fathers told us about when they said, "Did not the Lord bring us up from Egypt?" But now the Lord has abandoned us and put us into the hand of Midian.'"

This is powerful, and it is hard to not run off topic here. This verse can point out a few things that happened in our lives.

Let's set the stage here and understand that the moral of this passage is that the Israelites did evil in the eyes of the Lord, forsake Him, and worshiped various gods of the peoples around them (Baal).

The Israelites were practicing sin and idolatry but wanted to question why God had delivered them into the hands of the Midianites. I have two thoughts or things I would like to touch on.

The first one being:

1- We are just like the Israelites, practicing sin (different from sinning), and want to know why things are not going right in our lives. We like to blame the Enemy for all the issues in our lives, but truth be told, we bring most of the drama to ourselves because of our bad decisions. Stop giving the devil so much credit. We need to start being accountable for our own actions and behaviors. As followers of Christ, we must listen to the Lord; we must be obedient to what He is telling us. We, as humans, tend to sift through what we want to read, hear, or implement in our lives. The reason we do this is because what God is telling us or leading us to does not line up with our fleshly desires. If we fully listen to what the Lord tells us, we will have to change our ways, and for most of us, change is uncomfortable. It is easier to sit in sin and be comfortable in our chaos. We are called to be set apart from the ways of the world, so that will require us to make some tough decisions. We will have to close doors on some relationships that we know are not healthy, and we will have to politely decline some functions because we know that there will be behaviors we do not and will not take part in. We must stop asking God why things are not going the way we feel they should, but we know in our hearts that we are living a life where God is not first.

How can we expect to see God's wondrous works when, just like the Israelites, we are worshiping things other than God? It may look different than you think, and if you think that I am talking about a statue, a figure, I am not.

How many of us can go a day without vaping? That stick is your god!

How many of us cannot go a day without watching porn? That is your god!

How many of us cannot go a day without focusing on how much money we are going to make? There is your idol and your god!

We need to identify the idols in our lives, and as hard as it is to accept it, we need to knock them down and make Him first again.

We serve a jealous God, and He wants to be first in every aspect of our lives, from our decision-making, marriages, families, and finances.

A Few Quick Ways to Recognize the Idols in Our Lives:

> •Does it come before God?

> •Do you wake up and surf social media before thanking your Lord and Savior?

> •When you have not done it, had it, or watched it, do you have a challenging time functioning?

> •Is it all you can think of throughout your day?

After we identify those idols, we need to ask ourselves if we have that same insatiable desire for God's Word the same way we have it for that idol.

Now, let me speak on point two that I took from my reading.

When we bring it back to verse 12, Gideon is spoken to by an angel of the Lord, and the angel refers to Gideon as a mighty warrior. He also tells him that the Lord is with him. Now, Gideon, like most of us, began to question the Lord. We can tell in the verses before and after that Gideon did not see himself the way the Lord saw him, and in verse 13, he even questioned if the Lord was still with him. I am not sure about anyone else, but I can relate to him. There have been times in my life when I did not think I was qualified to do something, and then God showed up and showed off. I remember my friend telling me this many years ago: God does not call the qualified; He qualifies the called, and not because of our strength but

the power that resides in each one of us!

Romans 8:11:

"If the spirit of him who raised Jesus from the dead dwells in you, he who raised Christ Jesus from the dead will also give life to your mortal bodies through his spirit who dwells in you."

We must start seeing ourselves the way God sees us because we are enough, we are worthy, we are valuable, and we are mighty warriors.

Even after the Lord told him, he still doubted and said, "But I am the least of my family." We serve a mighty and powerful God, so what he should have said was, "I am the least of my family, BUT GOD has given me the power and authority. I felt less than, BUT GOD has filled my cup, and I am more than a conqueror."

We must STOP letting the Enemy continue to whisper lies in our ears. When he tries to whisper that you are not enough, that no one loves you, or that you are not good enough to be on the baseball team (yeah, the baseball team is personal), you shout back that you are a child of the highest GOD and that your value comes from Him and Him alone.

"You are the head and NOT the tail." —Deuteronomy 28:13 (AMP)

"And the Lord will make you the head (leader) and not the tail (follower); and you will be above only, and you will not be beneath, if you listen and

pay close attention to the commandments of the Lord your God, which I am commanding you today, to observe them care- fully."

"You were made on purpose for a purpose!" —Ephesians 2:10 (NKJV)

"For we are his workmanship, created in Christ Jesus for good works, which God prepared beforehand that we should walk in them."

1-Be Intentional on Reading the Word of God

Be in the Word, even if it starts as small as a verse a day. The Word of God is transformational, and when we are intentional about our time in the Word, we will see change in all areas of our lives because our hearts will be changed. There are so many things available to us that we have no excuse to not be in the Word. The Bible app reads to you, there are podcasts, and you can go on go on YouTube to find any sermon that you want to hear.

2-Start and End Your Day with Prayer

Stop overcomplicating this. Prayer is a conversation between you and your heavenly Father. You can start out by thanking Him that you woke up this morning, that your family is healthy, and that you have a roof over your head and all the things that we take for granted every day. Let Him know what you're struggling with. God hears every word that we speak and catches every one of our tears.

3-Get an Accountability Partner

This is not as easy as the other two things, believe it or not. The person you choose needs to be rooted in the Word of God and needs to be a person of integrity and good morals. This person needs to be emotionally and spiritually healthy. Your goals and values need to be in alignment. Your accountability partner should not be a single guy if you are married; you both have two different things and transparent) with your accountability partner. No matter what the situation is, you need to be able to confide in this person and know that what they tell you is for your best interest.

- W E E K 7 -

ARE YOU READY?

Key Verse:

1 Peter 1:13–16, NLT not practicing obedience? – "So prepare your minds for action and exercise self-control. Put all your hope in the gracious salvation that will come to you when Jesus Christ is revealed to the world. So you must live as God's obedient children. Don't slip back into your old ways of living to satisfy your own desires. You didn't know any better then. For the Scriptures say, 'You must be holy because I am holy.'"

1 Peter 1:13–16, NLT not practicing obedience? - "So prepare your minds for action and exercise self-control. Put all your hope in the gracious salvation that will come to you when Jesus Christ is revealed to the world. So you must live as God's obedient children. Don't slip back into your old ways of living to satisfy your own desires. You didn't know any better then. For the Scriptures say, 'You must be holy because I am holy.'"

- DAY 1 -

PREPARE FOR ACTION

Reflection Step: Reflect on what it means to prepare your mind for action. Consider the importance of equipping yourself spiritually. What distractions do you need to eliminate from your life?

Action Step: Spend time in prayer today, asking God to help you identify areas in your life that require preparation. Write down specific distractions to set aside.

1 Peter 1:13–16, NLT not practicing obedience? - "So prepare your minds for action and exercise self-control. Put all your hope in the gracious salvation that will come to you when Jesus Christ is revealed to the world. So you must live as God's obedient children. Don't slip back into your old ways of living to satisfy your own desires. You didn't know any better then. For the Scriptures say, 'You must be holy because I am holy.'"

- D A Y 2 -

PRACTICE SELF-CONTROL

Reflection Step: Self-control is vital for living out our faith. Reflect on situations where you've struggled with self-control and identify how you could have responded differently.

Action Step: Create a plan for an area where you need self-control. This could be setting boundaries with social media, unhealthy habits, or relationships that lead you astray.

1 Peter 1:13–16, NLT not practicing obedience? - "So prepare your minds for action and exercise self-control. Put all your hope in the gracious salvation that will come to you when Jesus Christ is revealed to the world. So you must live as God's obedient children. Don't slip back into your old ways of living to satisfy your own desires. You didn't know any better then. For the Scriptures say, 'You must be holy because I am holy.'"

- DAY 3 -

LIVE AS GOD'S OBEDIENT CHILD

Reflection Step: Obedience is a reflection of our relationship with God. Assess how you are living as a child of God. Are there areas that you are not being obedient?

Action Step: Write down one specific area of your life where you need to practice obedience. Commit to taking one concrete step toward change this week.

1 Peter 1:13–16, NLT not practicing obedience? - "So prepare your minds for action and exercise self-control. Put all your hope in the gracious salvation that will come to you when Jesus Christ is revealed to the world. So you must live as God's obedient children. Don't slip back into your old ways of living to satisfy your own desires. You didn't know any better then. For the Scriptures say, 'You must be holy because I am holy.'"

- D A Y 4 -

AVOID OLD WAYS

Reflection Step: Reflect on your past behaviors that do not align with your faith. What old habits are you tempted to slip back into?

Action Step: This is something that you may have read earlier, but it is an important step in your walk with Christ. Identify a supportive accountability partner. Reach out to them today and discuss the old habits you want to avoid. Set up a time to check in regularly.

1 Peter 1:13–16, NLT not practicing obedience? - "So prepare your minds for action and exercise self-control. Put all your hope in the gracious salvation that will come to you when Jesus Christ is revealed to the world. So you must live as God's obedient children. Don't slip back into your old ways of living to satisfy your own desires. You didn't know any better then. For the Scriptures say, 'You must be holy because I am holy.'"

- D A Y 5 -

SAFEGUARDS FOR YOUR FAITH

Reflection Step: God calls us to be holy in everything we do. Consider what safeguards you can put in place to help maintain your commitment to holiness.

Action Step: Create a list of practical safeguards—like daily prayer, attending small groups, or setting regular check-ins with your accountability partner. Implement at least one safeguard today.

1 Peter 1:13–16, NLT not practicing obedience? - "So prepare your minds for action and exercise self-control. Put all your hope in the gracious salvation that will come to you when Jesus Christ is revealed to the world. So you must live as God's obedient children. Don't slip back into your old ways of living to satisfy your own desires. You didn't know any better then. For the Scriptures say, 'You must be holy because I am holy.'"

- DAY 6 -

BE SENSITIVE TO HIS VOICE

Reflection Step: Being sensitive to the Holy Spirit's promptings is essential. Reflect on how you've responded to His call in your life.

Action Step: Spend intentional time in prayer, asking God to open your ears to His voice. Commit to acting on one prompting you receive this week.

1 Peter 1:13–16, NLT not practicing obedience? - "So prepare your minds for action and exercise self-control. Put all your hope in the gracious salvation that will come to you when Jesus Christ is revealed to the world. So you must live as God's obedient children. Don't slip back into your old ways of living to satisfy your own desires. You didn't know any better then. For the Scriptures say, 'You must be holy because I am holy.'"

- D A Y 7 -

LIVE FOR CHRIST

Reflection Step: This week's focus has been on living intentionally and obediently. Reflect on how you can ensure your life reflects Christ in all areas.

Action Step: Create a personal mission statement that embodies how you will live for Christ moving forward. Share it with your accountability partner for encouragement and support.

CLOSING PRAYER

Lord, As I finish this week of devotion, I want to thank You, God, for the growth I have experienced. Thank You for preparing my mind for action and living a life that glorifies You in all I do. Thank You for the grace, where I may not have hit the target, but see my heart and know my intentions. Lord, I glorify You. In Jesus's name, amen.

Author's Notes Based on 1 Peter 1:13–15 NLT

"So prepare your minds for action and exercise self-control. Put all your hope in the gracious salvation that will come to you when Jesus Christ is revealed to the world. So you must live as God's obedient children. Don't slip back into your old ways of living to satisfy your own desires. You didn't know any better then. But now you must be holy in everything you do, just as God who chose you is holy."

This is an amazing Scripture that was shared with me by a friend at work, and I wrote on it.

I'm going to touch base on this Scripture, piece by piece.

A Call to Action

Many of us read Scripture and repeat it, but Peter was calling us out and saying that we need to live it!

He was addressing a few things in these verses.

> 1–For us to prepare ourselves for action and practice self-control. *Prepare*: Make (someone) ready or able to do or deal with something (Oxford Languages).

What are we preparing for?

We are preparing for the second coming of Christ. We were commanded to know Him and make Him known as well as making disciples of all nations.

Acts of the Apostles 20:24 NLT

"But my life is worth nothing to me unless I use it for finishing the work assigned to me by the Lord Jesus—the work of telling others the Good News about the wonderful grace of God."

Matthew 28:16–20 NLT

"Then the eleven disciples left for Galilee, going to the mountain where Jesus had told them to go. When they saw him, they worshiped him—but some of them doubted! Jesus came and told his disciples, 'I have been given all authority in heaven and on earth. Therefore, go and make disciples

of all the nations, baptizing them in the name of the Father and the Son and the Holy Spirit. Teach these new disciples to obey all the commands I have given you. And be sure of this: I am with you always, even to the end of the age.'"

Peter was not telling us to go work out, hit the weights, and get some dance lessons in.

He was telling us to get our minds right, get our lives right, and prepare and equip ourselves with the Word of God, with consistent prayer and worship to our holy God. We need to turn off the distractions we allow in our lives; we are all guilty of it.

We are also preparing to take action against the spiritual warfare that is happening in front of our eyes. Many people take it lightly until it arrives at their front door with a crowbar. If we are not prepared, then the Enemy will have the upper hand. If we are prepared and trained for it, then we can fight back with God's Word, His promises, and HIS POWER. Let's take a peek at the other end of the spectrum. When not prepared, then we panic; we fall back into old ways of handling things like being angry, not coming to church, and maybe seeking things outside our home to soothe our pains or worries. Many fall far from God and become angry with Him. Why do we get mad at God? He told us these things would come; He warned us that we would have trouble. God has given us all the answers to the test, but when we don't study and fail, we want to be angry at Him.

Here is the next part that Peter was pointing out:

Live as God's Obedient Children

Since giving our lives to Christ and becoming followers of Christ, how many of us have been obedient?

I am not speaking about a slipup and then repenting for what we did. I believe Peter was speaking about knowing right from wrong and doing it anyway. Peter was speaking on the practicing of sin and bad behaviors.

As hard as it is, we must act, walk, and behave like the child of God He has called us to be.

We all know where we fall short in our own lives in this area, but if we need some examples, here we go.

- •Are we drinking and acting in a manner that is not glorifying to Christ?

- •Are we smoking and NOT attempting to stop?

- •Are we listening to things that are ungodly?

- • Are we flirting with people of the opposite sex?

When you know better, you're supposed to do better. We are supposed to learn from our mistakes and not continue to make the same ones over and over. We need to stop making excuses and blaming others for when we do something that is not in alignment with HIS Word.

I am aware that hanging with certain people will lead me into conversations I do not want to be in, so I do my best to bow out of these conversations or engagements to prevent me from doing exactly what Peter was warning us: not to fall back into our old ways of living and satisfying our own desires.

I am to live for CHRIST now. I am to stay steadfast and focused on the mission He has placed in front of me. I personally have to do whatever it takes to NOT fall back. If that means eliminating people, places, and things in my life that can possibly bring me back to who I was and take away from WHOSE I am, then so be it. If it is God's plan for them to be in my life, He will ordain it.

We have to put safeguards in place to help us in this walk, such as weekly calls set with an accountability partner and monthly coffee with that accountability partner. We can lie over the phone, but in person, our faces and body language will set off an alert to the other person, knowing something is off. When someone has an intimate friendship with you, they know your norm and can detect when you're not yourself.

Obedience also means to be sensitive to His voice and the Holy Spirit. Does He call you to pray for someone, but you do not because you're uncomfortable?

Is He calling you to love on someone, but you have neglected to because you don't think you can or the person is a little different than you?

Is He calling you to start a small group, but you feel it is an inconvenience?

"You didn't know any better then. But now you must be holy in everything you do, just as God who chose you is holy."

When we do not know better or have not been taught something, we can be faulted for missing the mark. Many of us did not have a godly man to replicate in our lives, so we have missed the mark, but now that we have the ultimate role model in our lives, we are called to be holy in all we do, just like God is holy.

In all we do, meaning the same Pauly you see on a Sunday should be the same Pauly you see on a Friday after pay day. When you hear a story about me, it should line up with the person you know from church and the men's group. I know that we all drop the ball and make mistakes—it is known that the only perfect man was Jesus, so I accept the one-offs that happen. I pray that the people in our lives know us well enough to know when that happens, it is a one-off, and they will look to see if we are okay and not hold it against us.

This may sound like perfection, but it's not; it is trying to be perfect in God's eyes and achieving excellence in the end.

A Few Takeaways:

> •Intentionality
>
> •Obedience
>
> •Know better, do better
>
> •Live for Christ and NOT self

May this devotional bring growth in all areas of your life and strengthen your relationship with Christ by the day!

God Bless you,

Paul DeZinna